"Julia's book i know the story of 't pond and watch the concentric circles move out to the shoreline.' This first book in this series gently guides the reader to the rationale for meditation and how the process begins. Julia has created an easy and understandable read and gratefully it is not full of jargon or complexities. I found it a joy to read and know others will have the same experience."

— Lloyd Field, PhD, author of *Business and the Buddha: Doing Good by Doing Well*

"This compact, sensible book sparkles with warmth and clarity. From enormous personal trauma, Julia has created enormous personal peace, and in this gentle guide, she shows us how. Her helpful tips for the beginner (also good reminders for experienced meditators) are presented without "religious robes," as she says. It makes this guide useable and giftable by those who prefer their inner explorations free of such affiliations. The moment I finished reading it, I could not wait to give it to a friend herself in need of peace. How glad I am that Julia is writing a series of these meditation guides, for she is a wise, encouraging friend for the ongoing journey."

— Irene O'Garden, author of *Women on Fire*

"Imagine you could give the gift of true happiness and contentment to anyone you love, to family or friend. With great simplicity and wise insightfulness this is what teacher and author Julia Hilton offers in this wonderful book on meditation. She begins with the simplest steps and leads you into a mature practice that will change your life and the lives of those you love while increasing your capacity for compassion exponentially. Believe me, it will heal and transform your whole world."

— Ron Starbuck, Poet/Author of *When Angels Are Born* and *Wheels Turning Inward*

"Dr. Julia Hilton has composed a thoughtful, insightful, and thorough exploration of the timeless practice of meditation for the beginner. Filled with personal anecdotes based on years of experience, the *Basics of Meditation* offers the perfect foundation for anyone interested in exploring the transformational nature of a contemplative way of life."

— Mark Trippetti, Creative Strategist, New York City

Basics of MEDITATION

The First Steps to Changing Your Mind and Your World

Julia Hilton, PhD

Blessings to You,
Julia

Basics of Meditation: The First Steps to Changing Your Mind and Your World

Copyright © 2014 Julia Hilton. All rights reserved. No part of this book may be reproduced or retransmitted in any form or by any means without the written permission of the publisher.

Published by Wheatmark®

1760 East River Road, Suite 145, Tucson, Arizona 85718 U.S.A.
www.wheatmark.com

ISBN: 978-1-60494-875-2 (paperback)
ISBN: 978-1-60494-886-8 (ebook)
LCCN: 2012948263

This book is dedicated to the life and service of Charles H. Hilton, Jr. (1948–2013). His presence in this world is sorely missed, but his wisdom, love, and honor will live on in my heart.

Acknowledgments

This book and the series of workshops on which it is based is the result of much collaborative work. I first want to thank my Buddhist philosophy teacher, Geshe Michael Roach, who changed my life when he held up a pen and asked, "What is this thing?" He not only taught me the deepest truths, but he saved me from depression and fear—I am eternally grateful.

Julia Hilton

Much of the content of this book is based on teachings from the Asian Classics Institute, and I'm grateful to all who have preserved that wisdom, including John Stillwell and John Brady.

Michael Kruse Craig has been a great friend and collaborator in this project. Special thanks to him, to Floriana Albi, and to Brain Pearson for their continued help developing MPI courses.

Lloyd Field, author of *Business and the Buddha*, and his wife, Joyce Field, offered invaluable advice. Moreover, they were very encouraging, allowing me to finish my work. Without them, this book would remain half-written.

Basics of Meditation

As this book is based on meditation classes I have taught, it seems to me the students in those classes are as much responsible for its content as I am. To all of you, I offer my deepest appreciation.

Finally, I thank my husband, Charles H. Hilton, Jr. He, above all, has taught me what it means to be a good person and to live up to my highest ideals.

Contents

Introduction 1
1. Why Meditate? 11
2. Preparing for Meditation 41
3. Stillness 57
4. Levels of Meditation Progress 73
5. Problems and Solutions 87
6. Ways of Knowing 109
7. Patterns 121
8. Reformatting 133
9. A Final Note 143
About Meditation Practice Institute 151
About the Author 153

Introduction

Meditation can and should be a very gentle process. Let's prove that by beginning with a very simple meditation. Where you are sitting, just get comfortable. Close your eyes (after reading this, of course) and count ten breaths. As you breathe, imagine your exhale is releasing everything you want to eliminate: negativity, anger, illness, etc. Imagine your inhale is bringing everything you want to you: positive energy, happiness, health, etc. Focus on one obstacle to get rid of and one joyful thought to bring in. You might exhale anxiety, for example, and inhale peacefulness. Just ten breaths. Go.

Bravo! You've just become a meditator.

In its most basic form, meditation is very simple. You've already done it. But it is also a deep and complex practice that can take years of study to understand and even more to master. This book, the first in a series intended to give a thorough explanation of meditation practice and practical applications for the modern world, will introduce you to the basics of meditation.

Basics of Meditation

My interest in meditation grew out of desperation. In 1999 I survived the crash of American Airlines flight 1420. That terrifying experience left me with serious psychological problems, including post-traumatic stress disorder, panic attacks, and dissociative disorder.

I spent five years searching for help through Western medicine and therapy, and while I did receive some amazing support from Western therapists, it wasn't enough. I still suffered from panic, nightmares, and insomnia—just a few of the many problems that plagued me. Perhaps my worst symptom from surviving the crash was fear that I was constantly in danger. Life was no longer a comfortable place; instead it posed dangerous threats. I remember one night being afraid to take out the garbage because it was dark, and I could not bring myself to face the unknown beyond my door.

One day, about five years after the crash while I was still struggling with panic and anxiety, a friend invited me to hear a Buddhist monk give a talk at a Christian church. The novelty of interfaith dialogue intrigued me. While I had been raised Christian, in the aftermath of the crash, I had become disillusioned with a God who allowed such tragedy. An eleven-year-old girl was one fatality of the crash, and I had seen her... it was unfathomable to me that a benevolent being with any control over this planet would allow such things to happen.

More out of curiosity than out of hope, I went to hear the talk. At the front of the church was a Western man, Geshe Michael Roach, in his Buddhist robes sitting on a cushion. He held up a pen in front of the audience and asked, "What is this thing?"

"A pen!" came calls from the crowd.

"But if I were to set it down on the floor, and a dog walked into the room," the monk continued, "what would it be to the dog?"

"A chew toy," responded the audience as the monk proceeded to chew on the pen.

"I ask you then," he said, very calmly with a most serene visage, "who's right?"

The audience gave various answers ranging from "both" to "neither."

"To a human, we're right," the monk said. "It's a pen. But to a dog, the dog is right—it's a chew toy. *And this proves that 'pen,' the quality of 'pen-ness,' is not inherent in this object—it is coming from the mind of the being who sees it.*"

I was amazed. I thought back to my experiences after the crash. One of the other survivors I had gotten to know in the hospital emergency room (because he was bleeding on me) had been physically hurt but not traumatized by the crash. In fact, he flew home to Alaska the next day. It would be years before I was able to walk onto an airplane again. And as I listened to the monk, I realized the truth of what he said. The world is not a terrifying place—the world is available to be wondrous or scary. *It's my mind that creates my experience.*

Basics of Meditation

I felt as if someone had finally given me a true diagnosis for my symptoms. My mind had been damaged by fear and trauma, and if I was going to heal, it would require mental exercise to change the way my mind worked—that mental exercise, explained the monk, is *meditation*.

Having found little help elsewhere, I decided to give his program a try. I began to study the art of meditation. I bought a cushion. I began a yoga program so I could train my body to sit cross-legged on the floor. And I started to meditate.

Eleven months later, I drove myself to the airport, I walked without fear (and without the aid of anti-anxiety medications) onto a plane, and I flew to Los Angeles to hear this monk speak again about the amazing benefits of meditation. By this time, I was not only a believer, but also a dedicated student.

That began what has now been a nine-year journey of in-depth study in Eastern philosophy and meditation techniques. When the people around me, including my mother, began to notice the changes in my level of happiness and my optimism for life, they asked me to teach them. I could think of no better gift to give another person than the techniques and skills they could use to improve their own mental health. And that is my motivation for writing this book. This book and others in this series are based on a meditation teacher-training program in which I translate ancient techniques of meditation into modern practices.

Basics of Meditation

Most information available about meditation today comes down to us through the world's great religions, including Buddhism, Islam, Hinduism, Judaism, and Christianity. But I've found that meditation taught as a secular practice (which can certainly deepen a person's personal faith) is much more accessible and helpful to everyone, regardless of religion, race, or ethnicity. Having studied in all of these traditions, most deeply in the Dalai Lama's lineage of Tibetan Buddhism, I have come to appreciate the value of each. However, *my belief is that meditation is powerful enough to shed its religious robes and walk out into the world on its own*—much the same as yoga has done—so that it can benefit people of any religion or belief.

Julia Hilton

Those who have studied meditation will notice a significant lack of religious doctrine in this series of books, and that is intentional. Because meditation can help *you*! Right where you are.

1
WHY MEDITATE?

As both a meditator and a teacher of meditation, I've found that motivation—actually getting myself and others to make the time to meditate—is my greatest challenge. I was teaching meditation at a health club in Tucson, Arizona. I had been teaching the class for two years when a student who I'd been instructing all that time walked up to me after class and said, "So I finally started meditating on my own, and it's *great*! It really works!"

I was shocked! It took him *two years*?

The principles of meditation, which teach us how our own mind is creating our experience of the world, are themselves life changing. Even if you never sit on a cushion, the things you will learn here will improve your life. But if you do get on the cushion (or chair), then the rewards of meditation are incredible. One of my teachers said it this way: "The amount of benefit you gain from meditation is directly proportional to the amount of time your butt touches the cushion (or chair)." *And it's true.*

Basics of Meditation

In order to motivate yourself to actually meditate, you must first understand the benefits and think about them often. I find one of the best ways to accomplish this is to do an Internet search for "benefits of meditation" or "meditation research." You will immediately find lots of scientific evidence about how meditation actually changes your brain and your body. Here are a few suggestions:

- Wikipedia offers an overview of current meditation research and links to many studies: http://en.wikipedia.org/wiki/Research_on_meditation

- Sara Lazar is a neuroscientist from Harvard University and publishes her team's work on this site: http://www.nmr.mgh.harvard.edu/~lazar/

- The Massachusetts Institute of Technology recently posted an article about meditation research in MIT News: http://web.mit.edu/newsoffice/2011/meditation-0505.html

There are two basic categories of the benefits of meditation: ordinary and extraordinary.

We'll start with the ordinary benefits:

1. Meditation increases your capacity to focus the mind on a chosen object. Your mind can focus on only one thought or mental object at a time.

Basics of Meditation

When we are unfocused, the mind jumps from one thing to another, rather than holding more than one object, as we sometimes think it does. Every first-time meditator will experience his or her mind jumping to other thoughts: lunch, a meeting, something that happened yesterday or will happen tomorrow. All of this mind-jumping creates unsteadiness and an inability to focus deeply or concentrate on the task at hand. This is sometimes referred to as "monkey-mind," and you can see why!

Perhaps more importantly, when we cannot control our minds, we are victims of our thoughts. An example might be the thought, "I'm not good enough" or "I'm stupid." These kinds of thoughts are often untrue. They are thoughts, and they may seem out of your control, but meditation can help you gain strength of mind to control them. If I asked someone with cancer (and I have), "Would you prefer to be thinking about your illness or enjoying the beauty of this moment?" He or she would most likely answer: "I would much rather enjoy this moment, the time that I have." But so often, we spend our time worrying or feeling afraid. If you could choose what to think about—for example, being able to focus on positive aspects of your life instead of negative—imagine how amazing your life would be!

2. Meditation increases creativity and insightfulness and opens new ways of thinking. Our minds are often like hamsters running around the same wheel over and over; however, when the mind is able to rest—in full awareness—it is more open to new ways of thinking, insights, and genuine creative thought. Through meditation practice we can learn to let go of old patterns of thought and break through inhibiting self-constraints that may be keeping us from finding new solutions, writing new songs, or creating new technologies.

3. Meditation creates peace of mind by reducing stress and anxiety and leads to better health, increased productivity,

and happiness. The wellness of our physical body is connected to the wellness of our mind. Consider as evidence the fact that when we are very upset, our breathing becomes shallow and erratic, but when we are calm and peaceful, our breath is even and light. Extensive research has proven that meditation—the practice of stilling and focusing the mind—has great physical benefits such as reduced heart rate, healthier blood pressure, and lower cholesterol. Additionally, when you are in a state of meditation and you're not thinking about the things that cause you anxiety, worry, and stress, you are much happier. If you train your mind

Basics of Meditation

in meditation, you will be better able to avoid getting angry or upset even in difficult situations.

These are just a few of the "ordinary" reasons to meditate. It's good for you. Simple as that.

And that's good enough reason to study and practice meditation! But let me also mention the "extraordinary" reason to study meditation.

We'll start with a simple demonstration that will take a few pages. Go through the next few pages slowly. Try to see the pattern emerging as you progress through the images. At some point, your mind will make meaning

Julia Hilton

of the lines you see. Give it a try and notice on which page you are able to see the meaning in these lines:

Basics of Meditation

Julia Hilton

Basics of Meditation

Julia Hilton

Basics of Meditation

LOVE

Julia Hilton

LOVE

Basics of Meditation

If you went slowly and tried to see the pattern, you probably saw *love* before this last page. Right?

Go back through the images and find where you saw *love* emerge for the first time.

The word *love* is not out there on the page waiting to be found. Your mind has taken a few lines and shaped them into a pattern that it recognizes—the word *love*. And with that small word comes an entire freight train full of meaning. That word and those meanings do not come to you from the outside world. They are coming from within you. Get it? Love is not out there; it's in *you*.

Go back through the images again. Now that you have found *love*, you will be able to see it in the first or second frame with no problem—not because *love* is out there, but because you now have a stronger pattern for love in your mind.

What this simple exercise proves is that your mind is receiving information from the world around you and is then—this is the important part—*making meaning based not on what you're seeing or hearing but based on your own mental patterns.* A person who doesn't speak English would neither see the word *love* emerge on the page, nor would they have the emotional response to that word that an English speaker has. What makes this extraordinary is that it proves—much as the Buddhist monk taught me so many years ago—that if I change my mental patterns, I will change my experience of the world.

Basics of Meditation

As I studied meditation, my personal experience of panic helped me understand these principles. I was on an airplane that was descending for landing, and I could feel my anxiety level rising. I was afraid. I looked around at the other passengers and saw that some were reading, some even laughing! Did they not know we were in danger? And then I realized, the plane landing was not scary to them. It was to me, not because of the situation but because of the patterns in my mind. And the only way for me to alleviate that fear? Change my mind!

Through months of intense meditation practice, I worked to change the patterns in my mind from those of fear and danger to joy and excitement. I won't tell you it was always easy—dedicated meditation practice is similar to a physical fitness routine; getting results requires rigorous work. But if you learn the practice by taking small steps, you can eventually accomplish great things.

Going back to our example of *love*. Yes, love is coming from the patterns in your mind. But we cannot force our minds to change patterns any more than I could force my body to not panic as I thought about flying. To prove this, turn back to image 2 of the love exercise above. Try to see *hate* there. Give yourself a moment and try to change what the word could be. It might seem impossible because your mind has already solidified what those lines will mean to you.

Basics of Meditation

Here's an image using the same lines in image 2 but with a few extra lines:

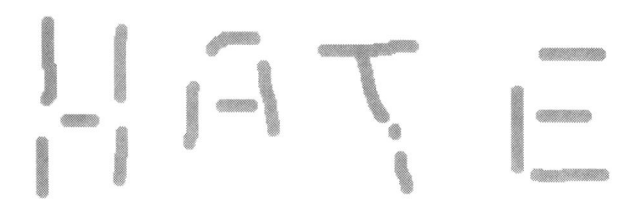

HATE

Julia Hilton

I'll include the original screen and its original conclusion for comparison:

Basics of Meditation

What this demonstration should prove to you is that the label we place on things, the meaning we make out of the dots and lines presented to us by our senses, depends not on what is "out there" but what is "in here."

In our current state, we are incapable of choosing love over hate or fear or peace. But if we practice meditation and strengthen our mind, we can change the patterns. We can fly in a 140,000-pound metal tube and feel complete panic at the possibility of crashing…or complete joy at the miracle of flying!

Every single object we encounter or event we experience has potential—the potential, for example, to be fearful or exciting.

Julia Hilton

I went to a movie recently with a friend. I thought it was shoddy, with bad acting and a sorry plot, while my friend thought it was wonderful and romantic. It reminded me of the truth that the movie was "available" to be good or bad depending on who was watching and the patterns in that person's mind.

Here's another example. Imagine you are sitting right now in your favorite place, be it a chaise longue on the beach or under a tree in the mountains. You love this place, right? But is it possible that another person could be miserable in the place you love? I know a woman who loves cold weather and snow. But I am from the desert, and the idea of shoveling snow or waiting for the ice to melt off my car's windshield is unpleasant to me. This simple example shows that it is not the cold or the snow that makes me uncomfortable. Rather, it is my mind, my mental patterns, that force me to feel the way I do.

While I prefer the sun (and if possible a beach), some people are very happy in snow. But here's the trick: were I stuck in a place that was cold, could I be happy there? Could I find a way to be grateful for what I had and feel joy in the situation? The answer is yes! But only if I can control my mind.

If I can control my mind, I can control my experience of the world. And wouldn't that be amazing? That's the extraordinary benefit meditation offers us.

To gain that kind of mental control takes a serious meditation practice. Meditation is to the mind what exercise is to the body. If you want to be able to run or ride a bike for miles, you have to train. You have to get stronger. Happiness is like a ten-mile hike. It is possible. But for some people it takes effort, it takes training. Meditation is the training that will give you the power to think and be what you want.

And we have to start somewhere.

If you've followed the suggestion at the beginning this book, you've already meditated. But there are some details that will help promote a stronger and more

Basics of Meditation

successful meditation practice. What follows are preparations for meditation—time-tested techniques to help you get the most out of your practice.

Julia Hilton

SUGGESTED MEDITATION:

- Get in a comfortable seated position.
- As you did in the beginning meditation, close your eyes (after reading this) and count ten breaths.
- As you breathe, imagine your exhale is releasing everything you want to eliminate: negativity, anger, illness, etc.
- Imagine your inhale is bringing everything you want to you: positive energy, happiness, health, etc.
- Focus on one obstacle to get rid of and one goodness to bring in. You might exhale illness, for example, and inhale health.
- Now that you're gaining some experience, once you've counted to ten, drop

Basics of Meditation

the counting and just focus on your breath for one full minute.

- Breathe out what you want to rid yourself of and breathe in what you need.

2
Preparing for Meditation

Place

You need to create a meditation space that is, as much as possible, quiet, clean, and special.

Meditation, especially for beginners, is

nearly impossible in a noisy or disruptive environment. Try to create a space where others won't bother you and noise is minimal—earplugs can really help with this. I have a dog that is very playful, but with a few simple lessons, he quickly learned to wait outside my meditation room, which is our spare bedroom. People can be taught like this as well. If you live with others, explain to them why you want to meditate and ask for a few minutes of quiet in the house. Another way to deal with this is to meditate in the morning before other family members wake up or to find a time after the kids have left for school. I know one woman who meditates in her car for twenty minutes before she goes into work—this is the only way she can guarantee herself no disruptions. Be creative when thinking about noise and distractions. Perhaps you could walk to a quiet place in the neighborhood or stop by a park on the way to work. In our hectic world, quiet is a rare and precious gem. See if you can find a piece of it for yourself.

Your meditation space should be clean. We'll talk more in later books about the connection between mind, body, and world, but what's important to know now is that they *are* connected, and you can affect one by affecting the other. Your environment is a reflection of your mind and vice versa, so having a clean, clear place to meditate will make it easier (and more fun) to work with your mind. If you have space, dedicate a whole room to your meditation. Clear out that junk you've been saving "just in case," and give yourself the gift of clean space. One of my friends uses a large closet in the back of her house. She can close the doors and have the space all to herself. If you don't have a lot of room, dedicate a corner or a small section of a room to meditation.

Making your meditation space special will also aid your practice (both in terms of helping motivate you to do your practice and making your practice more powerful). Add decorative touches to make the space beautiful (whatever that means to you), and include inspiring images. A picture of a beautiful flower or landscape can trigger a more peaceful state of mind, as can an image of someone you love. I have both in

Basics of Meditation

my meditation space. When I first began studying meditation, I was shocked to learn that there are few temples where Buddhists gather for their equivalent of "church." While large group temples do exist in most Buddhist cultures, every single person has a small temple in his or her own house. A woman I spoke with in Tibet was shocked to learn that Westerners don't have personal temples. She asked me, "Where do they do their daily practices?" I didn't have an answer. Your meditation space is a temple—built in honor of your own success and happiness.

Included in this space is your meditation seat. You need to find a meditation cushion or chair that is comfortable for you—our bodies are all different, and what is comfortable to one person can be simply painful to another. There are benefits to sitting cross-legged, such as a strong foundation and close connection to the earth. But the benefits are outweighed by the negatives if this causes you pain. Yoga and other exercise can help make your body more pliable for sitting meditation. In fact, according to the *Yoga Sutras* by Master Patanjali,[1] the goal of physical asana is to get the body in shape for meditation. You will not have a successful meditation session if you spend all of your time thinking about aching knees. I suggest you try out different cushions, benches, and chairs to find something that is conducive to both stillness and comfort. During

---

[1] Written over two thousand years ago, the *Yoga Sutras* by Master Patanjali is considered by many to be the most important historical text in the yoga tradition. The *Yoga Sutras* explain the eight limbs of yoga, which include a description of "asana" or the physical exercises that are the basis of most contemporary yoga.

meditation, whether it be a two-minute or a two-hour practice, your body should remain perfectly still. This is difficult to do if you are uncomfortable.

Investing in your practice (as in any activity) can be both fun and inspiring. So spend some time and spend some resources. Making your meditation space beautiful and comfortable will create a more powerful practice.

Time

There are two components to timing for meditation: time of day and duration of your practice.

The best time to meditate is when your mind is fresh and undisturbed. For most of us, this is first thing in the morning. But there are exceptions, and you may find a midday break or an evening practice more useful. For beginners, I suggest practicing in the morning before the worries and concerns of the day agitate your mind. It's also best to avoid trying to meditate when you're tired, such as at the end of the day and after a heavy meal, as both of these tend to make the mind very dull.

Whatever time you choose, try to pick one that can be *consistent* for you. I will tell you from experience that if you try to squeeze meditation in when you have a free moment, you will never have a free moment to do so! So designating a specific time of the day will allow you to actually find that time. Also based on experience, I can assure you that it will be difficult to schedule meditation into your day at first. But if you do so and actually start meditating on a regular basis, you will soon find yourself putting other agendas aside so that you can meditate.

One of the best ways to create time for meditation is to build that time into your current routine. Here are a few suggestions: just after your first cup of tea or coffee, before you turn on your phone/computer, just before or after you exercise, right after the kids leave for school, just before you leave for work. Attaching your meditation practice to something you already do habitually will help ease you into the practice.

Meditation should be done every day. To see results, you have to *be consistent and diligent with your practice.* That's why we start off with a very short practice, one you can commit to. Once you begin to see the results of your practice, fulfilling that commitment will be easy, as meditation will become as important as brushing your teeth, showering, or eating—and who forgets to eat?

Just like any other significant endeavor, it's best to start off slow. I recommend starting with a one- to two-minute practice and increasing that by one minute every week until you've reached at least twenty minutes. Some advanced meditators dedicate an hour or more every day to their practice. But if you start out trying to sit still and work with your mind for an hour, you'll give up as surely as an out-of-shape person would drop out of a marathon for which they had not trained.

Basics of Meditation

For those of you who are just beginning, I recommend the breath meditation described previously (i.e., breathing out negativity, breathing in goodness) for two minutes daily for the first week. Then increase that by one minute each week until you are up to five minutes. At that point, you will be ready to add "patterning" meditation, which we will discuss shortly.

Posture

While seating will vary greatly, there are some key aspects of how you sit that will affect your meditation. These are known in the Buddhist tradition as the Seven Points of Meditation Posture:

1. Legs must be comfortable and should be stable. If sitting on a cushion, use a cross-legged position (with support for your knees if necessary). If using a bench, legs are folded underneath you. If using a chair, feet should be firmly on the floor so there is no effort to holding your legs. In meditation we want to move beyond the body, and this will take time.
2. Eyes can either be closed or slightly open (if this isn't too distracting) and loosely unfocused on the floor in front of you.
3. Body must be very straight; the spine should feel like coins stacked in a tall pile. The position of your spine is very important to your ability

to meditate well. No slouching or overarching. If you are using a chair, either sit forward on the edge so that you have a straight spine or put a cushion behind your lower back.
4. Shoulders should be level, with your hands resting comfortably on your thighs or in your lap.
5. Head should be level, not turned up or down. Chin should be parallel to the ground.
6. Teeth and lips should be loose (no clenching).
7. Tongue should be lightly touching the upper palate behind your top front teeth: this helps reduce saliva so you'll have to swallow less frequently.

One additional point of posture is the breath. We try to always breathe through the nose (if that's not a problem physically), keeping our breath soft and thin but without a lot of effort. And we always count breaths beginning with an exhale and finishing with an inhale. There are two important reasons for that. First, counting breaths starting with an exhale is uncommon and so this keeps our attention more easily. Second, it's the opposite of natural flow; we are trying to change patterns in our mind, patterns that cause us unhappiness and illness, and this attention to reversing how we think about a breath is a first step in that direction.

Now that we've got the preparations covered, we're ready to meditate!

Basics of Meditation

Suggested Meditation:

- Gently close your eyes.
- Take a few deep, intentional breaths.
- Let the exhale relax your muscles, shoulders, lips, eyelids.
- Let the inhale lift and straighten your spine.
- Next count ten breaths, beginning with the exhale.
- Let go of negativities on the exhale, and bring in joy, health, and happiness on the inhale.
- Then for the next minute watch your thoughts—try to become an observer, a watcher of thoughts, and see if you can distinguish between the watcher and the thinker.

3
STILLNESS

Meditation helps improve our ability to control our minds by developing the "observer" and strengthening our awareness. *There are two parts of the mind: the part that thinks and the part that is aware of what we are thinking.* To understand this, think about the last time you were on a long drive. How much of that time were you aware of what you were doing, as in moving the wheel slightly to the left or right? Your mind must have known what it was doing, or you would have crashed. *But you were not aware of that thought process.* Sometimes we are very aware of our physical actions, but oftentimes, we feel as though we are on autopilot, and while we are driving, the main part of our mind is thinking about what we have to do later or what happened to us yesterday. One of our first goals of meditation is to strengthen that part of the mind that is our awareness.

This strength is developed through stillness or *shamatha* meditation. But it's important to keep in mind that stillness is just one half of the practice. While some traditions of meditation focus only on stillness—which is an important part of meditation practice, and what we'll study first because it is the foundation of mental strength and awareness—it is just part of a complete understanding of meditation.

I like to think of stillness meditation as being similar to the neutral gear in a car. If we want to stop going backward, it is necessary to move through neutral and put the car in drive to go forward. *In our meditation practice, moving forward means repatterning our thoughts through active meditative work.* However, this work requires the strength of mind and awareness that we gain through stillness. Both are necessary. And we'll discuss later in this book the second half of meditation practice, which is called insight or wisdom.

When beginning a meditation practice, it's important to fully understand the steps of stillness meditation. You cannot just sit down and try to hold your mind on an object and expect to make progress. This is one of the points at which meditation practice often fails! We hear that meditation will help us, so we sit down and try to not think about anything or to just watch our breath, but our minds do not stop. Soon we find ourselves thinking about what we want for lunch, how long we should sit there, how this is not working, how this couldn't possibly be helping us, that maybe we are just not able to do it… and on it goes.

Stillness meditation, like exercise, must build up slowly over time. No one goes from being a couch potato to running a marathon without some slow and consistent training.

Basics of Meditation

One of my favorite Zen sayings: no one blames the egg for not yet being a chicken. So we start where we are, we appreciate our current inability to control our mind, and we work slowly to increase that ability.

Stillness or shamatha simply means the ability to keep your mind on an object of your choice without interference. While it may sound easy, it is not! But it is possible, and with consistent practice, it can be developed. *Imagine what it would be like to be able to choose how to respond to any situation in life.* With this power of mind, we could eliminate anger, fear, sadness, and other negative emotions. This power is attainable, and it begins with the awareness of our thoughts cultivated by meditation.

In developing stillness, we start with the breath as an object because it is always available. A second reason for using the breath is that, while it is moving and changing, it is a very subtle object. Most of us already have the ability to stay focused on an object when that object is very active—watch people with their computers or smartphones. You will see serious focus! The problem is that their minds are depending on external stimuli to stay focused. Moving from an active object to a more subtle one increases our power of mind.

Let me give you an example to illustrate what I mean by this. Remember the last time you woke in the middle of the night worried about your health, a relationship, or work? You were plagued by thoughts of fear or worry, but at three in the morning there was nothing you could do about the problem. Nevertheless, you could not keep your mind from going over and over the problem, the possible outcomes, more fear, and more worry. Many people turn to distractions in order to stop these kinds of thoughts. Television, the Internet, movies, video games, or even conversation all serve to distract the mind from worry or fear, but they don't solve the problem. With the strength of mind and wisdom you gain from meditation, you will be able to stop those kinds of worry or fear with your own mental power. *And won't that be amazing?*

Now that we have some understanding of why stillness is important, let's talk about how to do it.

Julia Hilton

In its most basic form, stillness meditation means keeping the mind on the object of meditation—in this case the breath. It's important to understand that this may not be possible at first. Your mind will wander, and you'll find yourself making a grocery list or remembering a conversation you had yesterday. And that's okay—remember, *we have to begin where we are.* But each time we notice that the mind has left the object, we bring it back to the object, back to the breath, and it is that act of awareness—remembering the object and bringing the mind back—that builds our mental strength.

An important reminder for beginning meditators is that meditation practice is many things, but it is *not* yet another opportunity to criticize yourself! I hear students say things like, "I'm not good at this," or "I keep losing the object." And I suggest replacing those thoughts with ones like, "I'm getting better at this," or "I caught myself off the object. It's so great to have awareness!" Imagine that your mind is a five-year-old child learning to catch a ball. When she misses, we don't criticize her; we tell her it's okay and that she'll improve. And when she catches it, we jump for joy. Meditation should be like that.

Stillness Meditation Techniques

Begin your stillness meditation by placing the mind on the object of the breath. Counting the breath is a good way to do this because it helps you transition from an active (agitated) external world to a more focused internal world.

1. Close your eyes; find where you can feel the sensation of breath moving in and out of your body (preferably near the tip of your nose or upper lip, but if that's too subtle, you can use the movement of your chest or abdomen). Focus your attention on that point.

2. Count ten breaths beginning with the exhale. Breathe gently and easily, trying not to control the breath. (This practice will begin to strengthen the mind, because you will find it very difficult at first to watch the breath without changing it. As we develop the ability to observe the breath, we

strengthen the awareness part of our mind and reduce our dependence on the "thinker" part.)

3. If you lose count because you've started thinking about something else, simply start again at one. Some meditators go from one to three many times before they are able to stay on the object long enough to count ten breaths. And that's okay!

Once you've counted ten breaths (or tried a few times), move to an alternative technique of following the breath. Drop the counting, and, still using the breath as your focus, try different methods to keep your mind focused there:

- Temperature of breath—is it different for the inhale and the exhale?
- Length of breath—is it different for the inhale and the exhale?
- Pause in between breaths—can you find the pause where the breath turns around?
- If you are having a difficult time staying on the object, use labels such as *beginning, middle,* and *end* to keep your mind focused, but eventually try to drop those labels and observe the breath without language.

The last technique of stillness meditation is bringing the mind back. It is inevitable that we will lose the object of our meditation (e.g., breath), sometimes over and over again. We will find ourselves thinking about what we want to have for dinner or the work we have

Basics of Meditation

to get done that day. My mind loves to make lists of things, so I often catch myself going through a to-do list or a shopping list. We won't even notice that we've lost the object for a while, but then we will have a moment of awareness in which we catch our own mind. These moments are to be treasured and used as opportunities to bring the mind back to the object.

Never criticize yourself in your meditation practice. The mind becomes very subtle and impressionable during meditation, and your goal is to repattern your thoughts in a more healthy and happy way. Instead of pointing out flaws, use your meditation time to focus on your success. *Avoiding self-criticism in meditation is the first step in redefining your relationship with your own mind.* So when you notice you've lost the object, be happy that you've had a moment of awareness and simply bring the mind back. Gently. Joyfully.

Here are some additional tips about stillness meditation:

1. Start out slow.
2. Add one minute every week to gradually increase your capacity.
3. End your meditation before you get sleepy or agitated or feel pain in your body. Begin with just a few minutes.
4. Use a timer so that you don't have to worry about the time.
5. Watch for thoughts. If you're waiting for them, they tend to shy away.
6. Label intrusive thoughts with general

categories, such as past, present, future, or work, relationship, food, and then let them go.

7. Find joy in your practice and try to feel good about it. Examine, for example, the tingling sensation in your hands as your mind gets quieter. Always end your meditation with a smile and a positive thought, as this will inspire you to continue your practice.

Julia Hilton

Suggested Meditation:

- Set a timer for two minutes.
- Place the mind by counting ten breaths.
- Begin following the breath.
- Watch for thoughts and bring the mind back with joy when you catch yourself thinking about something else.
- Label intrusive thoughts and let them go.
- See if you can feel the pleasure in this practice, a sensation of tingling in your hands, or the happiness/peacefulness of your mind.
- When the timer goes off, smile.

4
LEVELS OF MEDITATION PROGRESS

Now that we know a little bit about getting ready for meditation (i.e., finding a quiet space that is appealing, choosing a comfortable seat, and making time for our practice) and a little about doing stillness meditation, what can we expect to happen?

I find it helpful to know the stages of meditation and what we can expect to have happen to our minds as we progress. This allows us to gauge where we are and to see where we're going.

Traditionally, there are nine levels of meditation progress (this comes from the Buddhist tradition but, as you will see, is quite general and applies to any style of meditation). In other words, as you progress in deepening your meditation practice, you will pass through nine stages of accomplishment:

Basics of Meditation

1. *Placing the mind*

    This is the first stage, where you place your mind on the object. The mind then leaves the object, and you try throughout your meditation to develop awareness of this movement and bring the mind back for brief periods of time. We begin to develop our ability to recall what we intended to do (e.g., watch the breath) and use this recollection to find our focus again. An ancient and very appropriate metaphor for these stages is that you are a trainer trying to tame a wild monkey. In stage one, the monkey runs chaotically around, totally out of control, while the trainer exercises patience and gently lets the monkey feel her presence.

2. *Placing the mind in a stream*

   In this second stage, you are able to keep your mind on the object for brief periods of time in between periods of distraction. In our analogy, the monkey now looks at the trainer for brief moments trying to understand.

3. *Fixation on the object*

   In this third stage, you begin developing continuity in your ability to stay on the object. This stage is characterized by longer periods of concentration and shorter periods of distraction. You gain the ability to use your awareness to catch your mind leaving the object and bring it back quickly and gently. Here the monkey has begun to pay some attention to the training techniques.

4. *Holding the object*

In the fourth stage, your awareness is becoming so strong that you no longer completely lose the object, but you still experience gross agitation (distraction) and dullness (sleepiness). This stage is characterized by a strong focus and strength of awareness, which may lead to subtle dullness. The monkey now pays attention to the trainer most of the time but is still a bit out of control.

5. *Bringing the mind under control*

Awareness to catch subtle dullness becomes very important at this fifth level. This is a difficult level to conquer because you *feel* like you have complete focus; the mind, because it is new to this ability to hold the object in an unbroken stream, will get dull and perhaps a bit lazy because our minds are not used to being quiet and focused without external stimuli. You have fixation and clarity, but not intensity. Now the monkey has gotten bored with its training and, while still doing what the trainer asks, has no enthusiasm.

6. *Making the mind peaceful*

   At this level you have mostly overcome subtle dullness, but you may still experience some agitation, where the mind is jumpy and overactive. You use your developed awareness to bring the mind down to stillness. *Your awareness is fully developed at this stage.* Now the monkey is trained and listens to the commands of its trainer with strong attention, but it still makes some mistakes and must be corrected.

7. *Making the mind totally peaceful*

   Because awareness (our ability to watch our mind) and recollection (our ability to remember our intention and keep the mind on our intended object of focus) are totally complete at this level, dullness and agitation rarely occur, but keeping the mind balanced and focused still requires effort. Now the monkey has learned its training very well and does most of its tricks immediately on command.

8. *Bringing the mind to single-pointed concentration*

At this level it takes some effort to put the mind on the object and keep it there, but then the mind remains effortlessly. At this point, the monkey requires a little instruction at first but then follows the trainer's commands without aid.

Basics of Meditation

9. *Placing the mind in deep meditation*
   In this ninth level, you have achieved total control over your mind. It becomes effortless to place your mind on the object and keep it there—you have completely tamed the monkey mind!

Here are some important ideas to note about these levels:

1. *Each individual's mind is unique.*
   You will progress through these stages at your own pace. Be patient and respect where you are while keeping an eye on the goal. But remember to never criticize yourself by saying, "I should be further along!"

If you continue to practice, you will improve, even if you remain at the same level for a time.

When I was starting out on my meditation journey, I went through a period of about six months where I suffered from terrible dullness. As soon as I sat on my cushion, I would start to fall asleep. It was almost painful to sit through group meditations where I had to fight to stay awake. It was as if my mind said, "Fine! If you're not going to let me roam around doing what I want, then I'll just sleep!" Meditating with other people at this stage was important for me because were it not for them, I would have gotten up and quit trying.

Basics of Meditation

There is great benefit to finding a group of like-minded people to practice with.

Once I overcame this period of dullness, the problem vanished and never returned. When you get stuck on one level, you have to remind yourself of the benefits of your practice and persevere! Doing so will be well worth it.

2. *You may move up and down on this scale on different days.*

One day you may feel you've finally reached level six only to fall back to fighting with losing the object in level two the following day. Don't worry. You can move up just as quickly. Many things affect our daily meditation practice, such as physical changes, emotional struggles, and job pressures. Just because you have to struggle today doesn't mean you've lost ground; it just means the conditions have changed and you're presented with a new opportunity to work with your mind.

If you feel your practice has stalled, review the causes and conditions: make sure you're doing all you can to create causes and conditions that are conducive to meditation. We've talked about the conditions above, which include the preparations.

Basics of Meditation

One final note about practicing meditation even when it seems difficult: what else are you going to do? Admit it, nothing else has worked. So what are you losing by giving yourself twenty minutes a day to work with your mind? Most people spend that much time a day watching television commercials that add no value to their lives.

At the very least, you are spending those twenty minutes thinking what you want (mostly) and gaining the benefit of a few minutes of peace and quiet. So when you get to the point where you think, "This isn't working!"—and I think most of us do—try to remember that. Give yourself a break. Then keep going!

5

Problems and Solutions

Not Meditating

Every meditator will experience problems as they start and progress through their practice, so I want to include some helpful tips about how to overcome these obstacles, starting with the most difficult one of all: not meditating.

Julia Hilton

Let's face it, starting good habits is hard. If it weren't so difficult to give up bad habits and pick up good ones, people would be lining up at the gyms instead of the fast-food restaurants, yoga studios would be more crowded than malls, and we'd all be riding bicycles to work! (Okay, maybe not, but you get the idea.)

The first step in overcoming the problem of not meditating is spending time going over the benefits of meditation. Read on the Internet about how helpful meditation can be. Dream about how nice it will be when you no longer have buttons that can be pushed.

I think what's most important when thinking about the benefits of meditation practice is realizing that in our current condition, *we are victims of our own minds.* We get angry, sad, afraid, upset, and depressed, and we have no control over these emotions. We live our lives desperately trying to get what we want and are rarely able to. When we happen to get what we want, the glory is often short-lived.

Think about the first person you had a crush on. Remember how badly you wanted him or her to talk to you and like you? Remember thinking, "If I had *that*, I would be happy!" And now, some years later, you might not even know that person anymore, or you might not like them. Did his or her attention really mean the difference between your happiness and lack thereof?

Julia Hilton

You can use this example when thinking about anything—cars, houses, vacations. *Most of us believe external conditions will bring us or give us happiness or peace of mind, but the truth is, happiness is a state of mind that is not dependent on anything.*

I like to think about Mother Theresa and Marilyn Monroe. Mother Theresa spent her time among the poorest and sickest people living in some of the worst conditions we Westerners can imagine. She was happy. She lived a long life. And more importantly, she was at peace with herself. Marilyn, on the other hand, had all the things we think we want—beauty, fame, wealth. And she was so unhappy she took her own life. What does that tell us about what is really important?

Basics of Meditation

When I confront this problem of not wanting to meditate, I think about what really matters. Is yet another television program or game of solitaire going to help me achieve a state of sustained happiness? Probably not! It might be distracting in the moment, but then, in the night, when I wake from a nightmare, I will be plagued by thoughts of fear and insecurity. Will twenty minutes of meditation help that? Absolutely! Because in that time, I can work on repatterning my own mind to be at peace, to be happy, to feel loved. And that's really what we all want.

If you are convinced then that meditation will help you (and it will!), think about the benefits. This will motivate you to do your practice.

Once you have that motivation, you will almost naturally begin to make time in your day for meditation. You will be able to dedicate three or five minutes to sitting still and strengthening your mind. That will lead to results. The next time a crazy driver pulls in front of you, you will not get so angry. You might even laugh at how silly it is to get angry at something like that. A broken glass in the kitchen becomes something funny and joyful instead of painful and ugly.

Those results will encourage your motivation, and in no time you'll be sitting for twenty minutes a day.

It's hard to keep up a new and healthy habit for long periods of time. Even dedicated meditators (and I know from personal experience!) "fall off their cushions" for days or weeks at a time. When I lose my practice—which means I don't take time to meditate for several days in a row, perhaps while traveling—I can feel the difference in the health of my mind. This is similar to how athletes who train daily feel the physical effects when they miss training for a period of time. If you realize it has been a week since you have meditated, bring to mind the benefits and this will help motivate you to start again.

Soon, meditation will become as important to you as brushing your teeth. You will have gained "practiced ease" and will be making excuses *to* meditate.

Losing the Object

Once you overcome the obstacle of not meditating, you will most certainly meet the next villain of meditation, which is losing the object. This problem happens while you're meditating. You sit down and start to count ten breaths only to suddenly find yourself planning what to say when your spouse gets home or what to have for lunch. Every meditator experiences this problem, and there is only one solution: when you realize that you are not focusing on your object of meditation, you can rejoice that you've had that moment of awareness and bring the mind back.

Joy is important here. Many failed attempts to develop a successful meditation practice result from self-criticism. You might catch yourself thinking about lunch, or a discussion, or something that happened ten years ago, or something that hasn't yet happened at all, and your critical mind will want to say something like, "Damn, you can't even count ten breaths. You're terrible at this! You should probably just give up, because this is hopeless." This is the mind we are trying to change. And the only tools we have to use against it are a smile, joy, and self-appreciation.

Next to not meditating, losing the object is the most difficult challenge. Why? Because your mind will tell you that you are failing if you lose the object, and this causes many of us to lose hope that we can gain anything from our efforts. But here's the reality: we are all victims of a wandering, out-of-control mind, and the only way we will overcome this is to develop strength of mind to rein in our thought processes. Each time you have even a brief moment of awareness that you have lost the object and bring the mind back, you have gained strength. And that's something to be happy about!

I like to compare meditation to physical exercise. We begin an exercise program not because we're already perfectly fit but because we want to be. The same is true with meditation and the mind. Though the physical work of lifting a weight or moving our legs is a challenge, it is that challenge that is making us stronger. Again, the same can be said of meditation and the mind.

See losing the object as a beautiful opportunity to gain strength, because it is in the awareness of that moment and the effort to bring our mind back to the object that we gain strength. Recall this strength when combating this obstacle.

Because meditation is done silently and internally, it's hard to get a grasp at first of what to expect. So I include here an example of a typical beginner's meditation:

> First, I create a pleasant space in which to meditate and then find a seat that is comfortable. I put a flower on the table next to me. I light some incense or a candle. Next, I sit down

and wiggle a bit to make sure I'm comfortable. Then I set my timer for three minutes, as I am just starting out.

I close my eyes. I focus my attention on my breath and begin to count. Exhale, inhale—one. Exhale, inhale—two.

Amy was pretty rude to me yesterday at lunch. I wonder if I should call her and see what's up. I wonder if I did something to make her mad. Last year when Sonja and I had that argument, it was all over nothing and...
I'm not focused on my breath. Damn it! Oh, wait, I'm supposed to be happy

about the awareness. Okay, cool. I've had a moment of awareness. I smile a little bit and focus on my breath.

Exhale, inhale—one. Exhale, inhale—two. Exhale, inhale—three.

I'm kind of hungry. I wonder if I should have leftovers for lunch or see if Alex wants to... Oh! Happy I've caught my mind before I lost count. Exhale, inhale—four.

My nose itches. I should scratch it. I'm not supposed to move; it will go away. Exhale, inhale—five.

And my knee hurts. Maybe I should meditate on a chair instead of a cushion.

Why would I ever think I could sit cross-legged for this long? This is impossible! I'll never be able to...Joy, awareness! Exhale, inhale—six.

No seriously, my knee really hurts! This is not doing any good. I'm in pain and I'm not good at this. It reminds me of when I was young and my dad wanted me to play baseball. I hated it. I was scared of the ball. Baseball is supposed to be fun, but it was awful and...

Oh, crap! I'm supposed to be meditating! Wait! I am meditating. Bring the mind back. It's okay. I'm making progress.
And the alarm sounds. Meditation success!

Basics of Meditation

I think many people have the misconception that meditation is supposed to be easy and/or peaceful. It can (and will) be both of those things. But in the beginning, a practitioner must make effort. It's hard to get the mind to slow down; it's hard to reach a state of peaceful contemplation. But it is possible. The strength we gain through battling the obstacle of losing the object will get us there.

Always remember to bring the mind back to the object with joy, grateful that you've had a moment of awareness. And always end your meditation session with a feeling of joy and success at having made the effort. Your effort will pay off, so be happy.

Julia Hilton

Dullness

The next obstacle most meditators will face is dullness. There are two kinds: gross dullness is a feeling of sleepiness; subtle dullness is a fogginess of mind that keeps us from being highly alert. Gross dullness reminds me of being in school when I was younger, tired from too much extracurricular activity and having to sit through a lecture on physics or literature in a room of two hundred other students. I would be so tired that my eyes would close, my head would slump to the side, and it was almost painful to pay attention to what was important.

Subtle dullness is similar to the zoning out we do while driving. We're able to keep the car on the road, but we aren't paying intense attention to the activity of driving. Mental dullness in both its forms is a formidable enemy that must be overcome if you are to succeed in meditation practice.

Dullness usually follows losing the object because once we gain enough control over the mind to stop its erratic wandering, the mind responds with, "OK, it must be nap time!" Like a petulant child, the mind will respond to your newfound control over wandering with, "Fine! I don't get to think about how angry I was at Jessica last month, so let me sleep!" But just as we can overcome losing the object by bringing the mind back with joy, we can (and must!) overcome dullness by brightening the mind.

The first tool to use against dullness is to bring joy to your practice. Think intentionally about how nice it is to have some time of quiet contemplation. Go back to the reason you wanted to meditate in the first place: think about the pain, the anger, the sickness, and how desperately you want to gain control over this problem. It will give your practice a sense of urgency that will help wake the mind and give it energy.

When I confronted this problem of dullness, I would think about my reason to meditate in vivid detail. I would bring to mind the pain and the suffering and how desperately I wanted to get beyond them. That gave me energy to complete my meditation sessions.

Basics of Meditation

Here's an analogy that might illustrate how this process works: Imagine you have decided you want to get up at five in the morning so you can exercise before work. The alarm rings at five, and you have two hours yet before you *really* have to get up; it would be so easy to hit the snooze button. This is your normal mind refusing to cooperate.

Now imagine it's five in the morning and the phone rings. Someone you love is ill and in the hospital and needs you. How easy is it then to get out of bed and get moving? A lot easier, right?

As meditators, we can use this innate ability to get moving by intentionally making our practice urgent. Think about the problems we face in life; think about the benefits of meditation and how much it can help us overcome these problems, and convince our mind how important it is.

The sad truth is our next life tragedy is waiting just around the corner for us. It might be a phone call about a loved one dying; it might be the doctor calling with a terminal diagnosis. We have no idea. But we do know it is coming. And to prepare for it, we need to meditate so that we can control this amazing machine that drives our world—our mind. *Use this truth to get your butt on the cushion and to get your mind to stay alert while you meditate.*

Basics of Meditation

If all that mental effort fails and you are just drowsy and dull, take some physical action. Brighten your room by adding light, cool your room down (warmth can increase dullness), stretch, move around, splash cold water on your face—then go back and try again. Avoid heavy meals before meditation and get plenty of sleep.

Dullness occurs because before we started the practice of meditation, our minds only stopped running in crazy circles when it turned off and went to sleep. There is a beautiful state of stillness that can be reached once we turn off the erratic mind while also keeping aware and awake. This takes effort but is well worth it.

Julia Hilton

Balancing between dullness and agitation (losing the object) is like holding a fragile teacup. Hold it too tightly and it will break. Hold it too loosely and it will fall. As you become skilled at meditation, you will become like a driver who knows instinctively how to move the steering wheel gently from side to side in order to stay in the correct lane. You will learn how to tighten the mind when it is agitated and how to loosen it when it is dull so that you can find perfect balance and intense concentration—and that's the place from which we can do serious work on our minds.

6
Ways of Knowing

Now that we have some understanding of stillness meditation, we'll move on to what I call *patterning meditation*. Patterning means you are actively working with the mind to change mental patterns; in a sense, we are moving from neutral into first gear.

Patterning meditation can be divided into three types:

1. *Review meditation*

    In this type of meditation, you go over something you've learned (like the nine levels of meditation progress discussed above) and deepen the pattern for that information in your mind. At this level we deal mainly with information or data, and we review it as a form of learning or study. Rather than listening to someone else, though, you are reviewing what you've learned in your own mind and memorizing the information deeply.

2. *Analytical meditation*

    In this type of meditation, you use logic to tease out the truth of something. This is a very important skill to learn because it brings us to a deeper level of understanding. Rather than just accepting information, in this type of meditation, we reason out things for ourselves. Someone might tell you, for example, that "all things change." Is this true? It's one thing to hear it and either understand or believe it, but it's a different thing altogether to come to know it through logical reasoning.

Here's a simple example of how beneficial this type of meditation can be. Suppose I give you a new car (I know, generous of me, right?), and I tell you that the car will run great for a while, perhaps a few years, but at some point it will need new tires or a new engine. Even knowing that information, you will probably be a little (or a lot) upset when the salesperson at the automotive store tells you that you need to invest a few hundred dollars in new tires or in a new engine. The level of frustration or pain you experience in this particular moment is due to your not having a deep *knowing* of the true nature of the car. You knew it as information, but you didn't *know* it as truth in your own mind. If you sat down, though, and meditated on the truth that the car is impermanent and will certainly need repair someday, when that day comes, you will simply be okay with the fact that you need to buy new tires. You will feel no frustration or pain at all.

And the same would be true if I were to tell you that this body you have will someday fail you. We all know that to be true, but do we have a deep awareness of that truth? Most of us don't. *Analytical meditation on the truth that we will die can give us great power to enjoy this moment that we have now, and a beautiful sense of peace and acceptance when things change.*

3. *Single-pointed focus meditation*

    This type of meditation is usually used in conjunction with analytical meditation and requires a solid foundation in meditation practice that allows you to maintain focus on an object. Single-pointed focus is used when you have an aha moment of realization and you try to hold that realization in your mind for as long as possible. *Stillness meditation is the training that allows us the strength of mind to be able to focus single-pointedly; analytical meditation is the training that brings us to the aha moment.*

We will cover all three of these modes of meditation more deeply as we continue to develop our meditation practice. For now, it's enough to know the three types are available as we begin our practice.

Why are these modes of meditation important? Because they connect to the three types of knowing, which are as follows:

Basics of Meditation

1. *The first level of knowing*

    Someone tells you something and you hear it. This is a low level of understanding something. It's like someone describing the Eiffel Tower to you. You have no immediate contact with the object, you just hear about the object.

2. *The second level of knowing*

    You logically try to understand (using deductive or inductive reasoning and analogy). Someone might say, imagine the highest skyscraper you've ever seen, and then imagine that it's just a shell made of steel bars—*that's* what the Eiffel Tower is like! Or they might even show you a picture, so you can see what it looks like on film. This is a deeper understanding that allows you to get a better understanding, but neither of these ways of knowing can give you an experience of the Eiffel Tower itself.

3. *The third level of knowing*
Direct experience—and once you've experienced something directly, you have this deep knowledge, this wisdom, about the object that is unlike the previous two. Once you've seen the Eiffel Tower in person, you have profound knowledge of it—knowledge that you cannot gain through descriptions or even pictures.

Meditation works through these levels to deepen your understanding and help you

Basics of Meditation

change mental patterns:

1. I can tell you, for example, that anger is harmful to you and has no benefit. And you could agree that this is true. But the first time someone cuts you off in traffic or says something unkind to you, you'll still get angry. You may know (on a surface level) that anger is not helpful or healthy, but that doesn't prevent anger.

2. Then we could talk about how anger increases your blood pressure, causes ulcers, leads to poor health and poor relationships, and serves no purpose. I can tell you that in any situation it is much better to be calm and compassionate because you can make

Julia Hilton

wiser decisions—even in the face of danger. You could research these truths and think about them. And then the next time someone cuts you off in traffic, you will pause (for a brief moment, perhaps) and realize anger isn't healthy, but you'll probably get upset anyway.

3. Then, you meditate on the fact that anger hurts no one but you. You then come to a deep realization of this truth and hold it in your mind single-pointedly based on the strength of your previous analysis. This truth becomes deeply ingrained in your mind, and you gain this knowledge and wisdom about the harmful

effects of anger. If you have that deep, meditative realization—if you see it for yourself directly (after many hours of meditating on it)—then the bad driver can no longer make you angry.

The example just given is an over-simplification, as gaining control of your anger or sadness takes long and dedicated practice. But it is possible.

SUGGESTED MEDITATION:

- Review what you've just read about anger.
- Then do an analytical meditation to see if you can find any benefits to anger.
- Think about the truth that if you are calm and reasonable, you can react better in any situation.
- If you get to some realization about the truth of anger, try to hold it single-pointedly for a few moments.

Bravo! You've just made progress toward changing uncontrollable patterns in your mind.

7
Patterns

We've talked a lot about why meditation is useful. But how does meditation actually work? As we've discussed, we experience the world the way we do because of patterns in our mind.

Julia Hilton

Look at this image of mountains. When it rains, where will the water run? In the canyons and not on the ridges.

Why?

Because of the patterns that have been created over many years—the entire life of the mountain. And the patterns of the life of the mountain were created by what came before in the earth's formation, and those patterns were created by what came before, etc.

Basics of Meditation

Your mind is just like the water in this example; in fact, we call the mind not a "thing" but a "mind-stream," and it is constantly moving and flowing. For example, it runs into grooves of happiness or pain not randomly, and certainly not by choice. If we had that kind of mental control who would get angry? Who would ever be depressed? Rather, the mind follows patterns just as water running down the mountains, as it has been patterned to do.

When I get on an airplane, my mind flows down this deep groove or pattern called fear. Not because the airplane is scary—the people around me might be completely indifferent to flying or even enjoying it—but because trauma (in my case, surviving a plane crash) or intense experiences create deep grooves.

Mental patterns can be deepened by both the intensity and repetition of an experience. Your mind is like a supercomputer that records every single instance of your life and files those experiences into patterns. Scientists have actually discovered that these patterns exist physically in the brain and determine what you will experience.

So two things are happening in every single moment of your life: you are experiencing, and you are reacting. At first, we can't change the experience—we use meditation practice and strength of mind to begin to alter our reaction.

The beauty of this is, as our reactions change, so do the patterns, and thus we affect not just our reactions but the experiences themselves.

Here's an example:

> The plane is about to land, and it's scary! I'm anxious and upset.
>
> But I understand that my mind is creating *scary*, so I'll slow down my breathing and work to convince myself that I'm safe.
>
> I feel better. The plane is still scary, but I'm no longer anxious and upset.
>
> After much effort to control my mental patterns, the plane really isn't that scary—it's actually kind of exciting!

Of course, changing our experience doesn't always happen so easily, but over time it is very possible!

The point of meditation is not to learn to put up with negativities or things that are irritating, but to eliminate them. We start by changing our reaction, but the goal is to eliminate negative experiences completely.

To illustrate this more fully, we're going to take a moment of irritation and explain what's really going on:

1. Irritating person says, "You're stupid."
2. Before learning about the mind and developing our awareness, we think this is a cause. It's not! It's actually a result. If we hadn't created the pattern

of "someone calling me stupid" in our minds, we would not see it.

3. But we haven't learned that yet, and so we react (the second action of the mind) by getting angry, and the natural response is to say, "No! You're stupid!"

4. What's actually happened is we've just deepened the "stupid" pattern in our mind.

5. The only way to get rid of "stupid" (or ugly or sad or any negative emotion) is to eliminate that pattern. Because that is the true cause.

Mental patterns are created in three ways:

1. By what we think
2. By what we do

3. By what we say

Every time we get angry, we deepen the pattern for anger in our minds, and we deepen the pattern of seeing things that make us angry. *These are actually both the result of the same mental process.* As we discussed previously, our minds create anger and hate, and they also create what feels like an involuntary reaction to them. Likewise, our minds are responsible for generating the sense that something is good as well as our reaction to that goodness.

There are two ways to change patterns in our minds. The *first* is to change the way we think, speak, and act: we work to behave differently in the world, and this changes our mental patterns. Here's an example: suppose you are a person who feels financial constraints. It doesn't matter how much money you actually have, you feel like it's not enough to cover the bills and other life expenses. The feeling of not having enough is not just a physical reality; it is more importantly a mental pattern.

Many people with plenty of income find themselves struggling to make ends meet. At the same time, there are many people who have less money and feel very comfortable with their financial status. The amount of money you have does *not* equate to feeling financially secure, because the feeling of security is a mental pattern. To change this pattern from one of need to one of security with this first method requires that we begin to develop a practice of generosity in our thoughts, speech, and actions. Every time you offer to help someone else with financial needs using thoughts, words, or deeds, you create a new pattern in your mind for wealth. You donate five dollars to the Humane Society, and your mind creates a new pattern of "I have enough to share."

The *second* way to change thought patterns is to sit down on our meditation cushions (or chairs) and intentionally create new patterns. Maxwell Maltz pioneered research about what he called "psycho-cybernetics." His research showed that a group of students who mentally practiced shooting basketballs improved in actual practice nearly as much as those who physically practiced every day. His work and other scientific studies prove that working with the mind in meditation makes significant changes in our physical reality.

8
REFORMATTING

We're going to cover one type of meditation that can help you change mental patterns very quickly. It's a little like reformatting a computer hard drive. For this type of meditation to be effective, you have to understand how mental patterns work. You see pain not as a cause of your mental unhappiness but as a result of previous patterns of pain (those you've caused others and those you've created in your mind). You don't have to break someone else's arm to see that happening to you. You simply have the thought, "Oh, I hope they fall!" and the pattern is created.

One characteristic of mental patterns is that they are capable of growing significantly. The Grand Canyon is about three miles straight down (or ten miles if hiking down its twisting trails). When you get to the bottom, the Colorado River that created this huge canyon is only a few feet deep. The continued path of just a small amount of water can create deep crevices in the earth, just as small repeated mental patterns can cause big results.

Patterns in the mind are like a tiny acorn that becomes a huge oak tree. So you can't discount the truth of mental patterns by saying, "I've never done that to anyone!" We have created the causes to see both happiness and pain in our world in some small way—or we wouldn't see it happening to us. The good news is we need only make small, consistent efforts at changing the patterns in our minds to create significant results.

For this meditation, you choose the negative thing(s) you want to eliminate from your life (e.g., sickness, poverty, sadness), and you practice taking those negativities away from others for their benefit. Then you choose the positive thing(s) you want to bring into your life (e.g., health, joy, wealth, love), and you practice intentionally giving those things to others to create patterns for these things in your own mind.

This is an extensive and elaborate meditation. I suggest you spend some time doing review meditations on the steps so you'll have a clear idea of what to do during the meditation. You can also break this meditation into two separate sessions, "taking" and "giving."

If you take the time to practice this meditation, it will become very easy and will create new and positive patterns in your mind. So don't be discouraged by the details!

Steps for "Taking" Meditation

1. Close your eyes and take a few deep breaths; count ten breaths.
2. Think for a moment about something in your life you don't like. It could be

Basics of Meditation

a habit, a thought process, physical pain, a troubled relationship—just pick one thing for this meditation.

3. Now find someone else in your world who also has this problem. Try to visualize her clearly and see the pain on her face as she suffers with this problem.

4. Now decide that (in order to change the patterns in your own mind) you want to take this pain away from her and destroy it. This determination to change patterns in your own mind is your wisdom. And we visualize it physically as a tiny, bright diamond right at the center of your body, about the level of your chest just in front of your spine.

5. Now look back to this person who is in pain. See her problem as a black smoke that fills her body. As you breathe, use your breath to draw that black smoke out of her through her nose. See the pain as a small black cloud that you are drawing out of her on your breath. It forms into a small, thick black ball of smoke just in front of you.

6. On the next breath, take on that pain in order to destroy it. Imagine breathing it in through your own nose, into your own body, and draw it down to your heart center, where it is destroyed when it touches the diamond of your wisdom.

7. Make sure you see the darkness and pain totally destroyed. Then just sit for a moment and be happy about what you've done. Deepen the pattern in your mind by rejoicing about how you've destroyed that pattern of pain.

Remember, we work with our mind in meditation to change patterns because it is very difficult to change our patterns of activity in the world—but we have to work on both. The good thing about working with the mind is we are limited not by our current physical reality but only by our imagination. As it is now, I am very limited in what I can do for another person who is in pain. I can listen and even take someone to the doctor, but I have no power to heal him. In your meditation, however, you *can* do it through imagination! And this creates powerful mental patterns for health.

Steps for "Giving" Meditation

1. Close your eyes and take a few deep breaths; count ten breaths.
2. Think for a moment about what you want. It doesn't have to be a lofty goal; it can be something simple: I want to be happy. As you continue to practice this meditation, expand and deepen your goals.
3. Then think about someone else who also needs this thing—just one other person you know who is unhappy. Try

to visualize him sitting somewhere alone.

4. Now imagine that you can give him happiness. The more detailed your imagination, the stronger the patterns you create.

5. Next, expand this visualization by imagining you could replicate this act of giving for every single person on the planet. Visualize light coming out of your heart center (from that diamond of wisdom), and carried on those rays of light are seeds of happiness for everyone. Try to stay focused and give those things away. Watch how happy the people are who receive them. See their joy and really

believe for just this moment that you are actually giving them happiness.

6. Now sit back and rejoice at having done this great act of giving. Let the patterns of having given away what you want sink deep into your mind.

As your ability to meditate increases, you can combine these two meditations into one session, first taking away pain from one person and giving him what he wants, and then expanding it to include everyone who is in pain or in need. This creates powerful patterns. And it is the single most effective way of changing patterns in your own mind.

9

A Final Note

In the meditation tradition, we distinguish between the "causes" and "conditions" of a successful meditation practice. Causes work; conditions help.

Here's a simple example of that. To understand this division, we'll use the example of an aspirin. We take aspirin when we have a headache. Sometimes it works, and sometimes it doesn't. So we can't say aspirin is the "cause" of ending a headache, because if it were a cause, it would work all the time. And yet, sometimes the aspirin does work, so we can say it is a "condition" that can aid in getting rid of headaches.

So what then is a cause? If a thing is a cause, it must produce the same result 100 percent of the time. A lettuce seed is a cause for a lettuce plant because 100 percent of the time, if you plant a lettuce seed, you will get a lettuce plant (if it's cultivated properly), and at *no* time will a corn plant just randomly grow from that seed.

Aspirin cannot be the cause of eliminating a headache because it doesn't work 100 percent of the time. Instead, aspirin is a condition that can help the headache go away.

Do you still take the aspirin? Of course! You still go to the doctor if you're sick, but you recognize that the doctor has only a chance of helping you. If you do your giving and taking meditations well and consistently, you create the patterns in your mind to see medicine working.

There are some important conditions that will help our meditation practice; we've already covered some of them:

- Find/create a space that is conducive for meditation; make it nice.
- Find a consistent time in which to meditate.
- Learn the proper techniques of medita-

tion by reviewing what we've covered in this book.

- Reduce your wants for material things—things you think will make you happy but really don't. Do you really think the new car will make you happy? It may for a week or a month, but then it's old. It's great to have nice things, but don't place your hope for happiness in them. Remember that true happiness will come from your success at meditation practice—put that first on your list of priorities!
- Cultivate a sense of contentment and appreciation for what we have.
- Avoid overstimulation and excessive busyness. As people dedicated to meditation, we might have to make some decisions. Is television really important enough to

spend hours a day on? Meditators need to reduce stimulation. Spend some quiet time in the morning after your meditation practice and before you turn on the computer. Sit on the porch or couch for a few minutes in silence. Learn to slow down and do one thing at a time. Eat instead of eating and texting. Drive instead of driving and talking on the phone. Develop single-pointed focus in your life as much as possible.

- As best you can, live a life of integrity. Try to treat others as you would like to be treated; it's amazing how well this works!

These are conditions. They will help you develop a stronger meditation practice. But to truly be successful in meditation, you must create patterns in your mind for mental health by helping and encouraging other people in whatever way possible. Encourage others in their meditation practice; help them feel less busy and stressed. Take a friend to coffee and offer some advice on how to deal with problems in his or her life. Give meditation success away in your own meditation. This will create patterns of meditative success.

The birth of a canyon is a small trickle of water led down a certain path. And the birth of happiness, health, and success is a small mental pattern repeated over and over again. Meditation gives you the power to control the river of your mind—to lead it into patterns of goodness and joy.

Basics of Meditation

Ultimate success at meditation will take years of study and practice, and when you're ready, start in on book two of this series. But it all starts with one minute. Right now.

About Meditation Practice Institute

The mission of Meditation Practice Institute is to enrich the lives of individuals and the success of organizations and businesses by providing meditation instruction that is founded on ancient tradition and tailored to meet contemporary needs. We further aim to deepen the effectiveness of meditation instruction through an advanced teacher training and certification program. This program is ongoing and available online.

For further information, contact Meditation Practice Institute online at:

ItsMoreThanYouThink.org

or by email at:

info@meditationpracticeinstitute.org.

About the Author

Julia Ferganchick Hilton, PhD, earned advanced degrees in writing, language theory and philosophy from the University of Arizona. She taught university-level philosophy, writing, and linguistics courses, and gave national presentations about language theory and practice during her career as a college professor (1992–2001).

Julia's nationally-funded research focused on the nature of language acquisition and the influences of technology on literacy. During this time, she also started a small business, a café/bookstore, which she ran successfully in Little Rock, Arkansas.

In 1999 she survived a major airline crash, which set her on a new course of study about how we deal with trauma and life.

About the Author

Julia began a serious practice of meditation in 2005. She completed the Asian Classics Institute's extensive program of Buddhist philosophy, and traveled to Europe, Asia, and India to further her studies. In 2007 she spent two months volunteering and studying in a remote monastery of the Kagyu lineage in eastern Tibet.

She completed advanced studies in meditation and eastern philosophy at Diamond Mountain University, and has completed certification in the Yoga Studies Institute Classics of Yoga and Tibetan Heart Yoga programs.

In 2006 she began teaching meditation regularly both in her hometown of Tucson, Arizona, and throughout the world. Julia specializes in teaching meditation practices that are accessible and beneficial to a wide

About the Author

range of people who seek to improve their lives.

Julia cared for her husband, Charles Hilton, after his diagnosis of terminal cancer in 2012 with the help of home hospice. During that time, Julia herself was diagnosed with breast cancer and the BRCA 1 gene mutation. She underwent a radical double mastectomy in April 2013. She now uses her experiences as a cancer survivor and meditation as a basis for her writing, which can be found on her blog: http://prajnaja.wordpress.com.

Contact Julia at:
julia@meditationpracticeinstitute.org.